SDA

Simply Digital Art™

This password book belongs to:

Notes

1

2

3

4

5

6

7

A

WEBSITE	USER NAME	PASSWORD

WEBSITE	USER NAME	PASSWORD

WEBSITE	USER NAME	PASSWORD

Notes:

A

WEBSITE	USER NAME	PASSWORD

WEBSITE	USER NAME	PASSWORD

WEBSITE	USER NAME	PASSWORD

Notes:

A

WEBSITE	USER NAME	PASSWORD

WEBSITE	USER NAME	PASSWORD

WEBSITE	USER NAME	PASSWORD

Notes:

A

WEBSITE USER NAME PASSWORD

WEBSITE USER NAME PASSWORD

WEBSITE USER NAME PASSWORD

Notes:

B

WEBSITE	USER NAME	PASSWORD

WEBSITE	USER NAME	PASSWORD

WEBSITE	USER NAME	PASSWORD

Notes:

B

WEBSITE | USER NAME | PASSWORD

WEBSITE | USER NAME | PASSWORD

WEBSITE | USER NAME | PASSWORD

Notes:

B

WEBSITE	USER NAME	PASSWORD

WEBSITE	USER NAME	PASSWORD

WEBSITE	USER NAME	PASSWORD

Notes:

B

WEBSITE | USER NAME | PASSWORD

WEBSITE | USER NAME | PASSWORD

WEBSITE | USER NAME | PASSWORD

Notes:

C

WEBSITE	USER NAME	PASSWORD

WEBSITE	USER NAME	PASSWORD

WEBSITE	USER NAME	PASSWORD

Notes:

C

WEBSITE	USER NAME	PASSWORD

WEBSITE	USER NAME	PASSWORD

WEBSITE	USER NAME	PASSWORD

Notes:

C

WEBSITE	USER NAME	PASSWORD

WEBSITE	USER NAME	PASSWORD

WEBSITE	USER NAME	PASSWORD

Notes:

C

WEBSITE USER NAME PASSWORD

WEBSITE USER NAME PASSWORD

WEBSITE USER NAME PASSWORD

Notes:

D

WEBSITE	USER NAME	PASSWORD

WEBSITE	USER NAME	PASSWORD

WEBSITE	USER NAME	PASSWORD

Notes:

D

WEBSITE	USER NAME	PASSWORD

WEBSITE	USER NAME	PASSWORD

WEBSITE	USER NAME	PASSWORD

Notes:

D

WEBSITE	USER NAME	PASSWORD

WEBSITE	USER NAME	PASSWORD

WEBSITE	USER NAME	PASSWORD

Notes:

D

WEBSITE	USER NAME	PASSWORD

WEBSITE	USER NAME	PASSWORD

WEBSITE	USER NAME	PASSWORD

Notes:

D

WEBSITE	USER NAME	PASSWORD

WEBSITE	USER NAME	PASSWORD

WEBSITE	USER NAME	PASSWORD

Notes:

E

WEBSITE	USER NAME	PASSWORD

WEBSITE	USER NAME	PASSWORD

WEBSITE	USER NAME	PASSWORD

Notes:

E

WEBSITE	USER NAME	PASSWORD

WEBSITE	USER NAME	PASSWORD

WEBSITE	USER NAME	PASSWORD

Notes:

E

WEBSITE	USER NAME	PASSWORD

WEBSITE	USER NAME	PASSWORD

WEBSITE	USER NAME	PASSWORD

Notes:

E

WEBSITE	USER NAME	PASSWORD

WEBSITE	USER NAME	PASSWORD

WEBSITE	USER NAME	PASSWORD

Notes:

F

WEBSITE	USER NAME	PASSWORD

WEBSITE	USER NAME	PASSWORD

WEBSITE	USER NAME	PASSWORD

Notes:

F

WEBSITE	USER NAME	PASSWORD

WEBSITE	USER NAME	PASSWORD

WEBSITE	USER NAME	PASSWORD

Notes:

F

WEBSITE	USER NAME	PASSWORD

WEBSITE	USER NAME	PASSWORD

WEBSITE	USER NAME	PASSWORD

Notes:

F

WEBSITE	USER NAME	PASSWORD

WEBSITE	USER NAME	PASSWORD

WEBSITE	USER NAME	PASSWORD

Notes:

G

WEBSITE	USER NAME	PASSWORD

WEBSITE	USER NAME	PASSWORD

WEBSITE	USER NAME	PASSWORD

Notes:

G

WEBSITE	USER NAME	PASSWORD

WEBSITE	USER NAME	PASSWORD

WEBSITE	USER NAME	PASSWORD

Notes:

G

WEBSITE	USER NAME	PASSWORD

WEBSITE	USER NAME	PASSWORD

WEBSITE	USER NAME	PASSWORD

Notes:

G

WEBSITE	USER NAME	PASSWORD

WEBSITE	USER NAME	PASSWORD

WEBSITE	USER NAME	PASSWORD

Notes:

H

WEBSITE	USER NAME	PASSWORD

WEBSITE	USER NAME	PASSWORD

WEBSITE	USER NAME	PASSWORD

Notes:

H

WEBSITE	USER NAME	PASSWORD

WEBSITE	USER NAME	PASSWORD

WEBSITE	USER NAME	PASSWORD

Notes:

H

WEBSITE	USER NAME	PASSWORD

WEBSITE	USER NAME	PASSWORD

WEBSITE	USER NAME	PASSWORD

Notes:

H

WEBSITE	USER NAME	PASSWORD

WEBSITE	USER NAME	PASSWORD

WEBSITE	USER NAME	PASSWORD

Notes:

WEBSITE	USER NAME	PASSWORD

WEBSITE	USER NAME	PASSWORD

WEBSITE	USER NAME	PASSWORD

Notes:

WEBSITE	USER NAME	PASSWORD

WEBSITE	USER NAME	PASSWORD

WEBSITE	USER NAME	PASSWORD

Notes:

WEBSITE	USER NAME	PASSWORD

WEBSITE	USER NAME	PASSWORD

WEBSITE	USER NAME	PASSWORD

Notes:

WEBSITE	USER NAME	PASSWORD

WEBSITE	USER NAME	PASSWORD

WEBSITE	USER NAME	PASSWORD

Notes:

J

WEBSITE	USER NAME	PASSWORD

WEBSITE	USER NAME	PASSWORD

WEBSITE	USER NAME	PASSWORD

Notes:

J

WEBSITE	USER NAME	PASSWORD

WEBSITE	USER NAME	PASSWORD

WEBSITE	USER NAME	PASSWORD

Notes:

J

WEBSITE	USER NAME	PASSWORD

WEBSITE	USER NAME	PASSWORD

WEBSITE	USER NAME	PASSWORD

Notes:

J

WEBSITE	USER NAME	PASSWORD

WEBSITE	USER NAME	PASSWORD

WEBSITE	USER NAME	PASSWORD

Notes:

J

WEBSITE	USER NAME	PASSWORD

WEBSITE	USER NAME	PASSWORD

WEBSITE	USER NAME	PASSWORD

Notes:

K

WEBSITE	USER NAME	PASSWORD

WEBSITE	USER NAME	PASSWORD

WEBSITE	USER NAME	PASSWORD

Notes:

K

WEBSITE	USER NAME	PASSWORD

WEBSITE	USER NAME	PASSWORD

WEBSITE	USER NAME	PASSWORD

Notes:

K

WEBSITE	USER NAME	PASSWORD

WEBSITE	USER NAME	PASSWORD

WEBSITE	USER NAME	PASSWORD

Notes:

K

WEBSITE	USER NAME	PASSWORD

WEBSITE	USER NAME	PASSWORD

WEBSITE	USER NAME	PASSWORD

Notes:

L

WEBSITE USER NAME PASSWORD

WEBSITE USER NAME PASSWORD

WEBSITE USER NAME PASSWORD

Notes:

L

WEBSITE	USER NAME	PASSWORD

WEBSITE	USER NAME	PASSWORD

WEBSITE	USER NAME	PASSWORD

Notes:

L

WEBSITE	USER NAME	PASSWORD

WEBSITE	USER NAME	PASSWORD

WEBSITE	USER NAME	PASSWORD

Notes:

L

WEBSITE	USER NAME	PASSWORD

WEBSITE	USER NAME	PASSWORD

WEBSITE	USER NAME	PASSWORD

Notes:

M

WEBSITE	USER NAME	PASSWORD

WEBSITE	USER NAME	PASSWORD

WEBSITE	USER NAME	PASSWORD

Notes:

M

WEBSITE	USER NAME	PASSWORD

WEBSITE	USER NAME	PASSWORD

WEBSITE	USER NAME	PASSWORD

Notes:

M

WEBSITE	USER NAME	PASSWORD

WEBSITE	USER NAME	PASSWORD

WEBSITE	USER NAME	PASSWORD

Notes:

M

WEBSITE	USER NAME	PASSWORD

WEBSITE	USER NAME	PASSWORD

WEBSITE	USER NAME	PASSWORD

Notes:

N

WEBSITE	USER NAME	PASSWORD

WEBSITE	USER NAME	PASSWORD

WEBSITE	USER NAME	PASSWORD

Notes:

N

WEBSITE	USER NAME	PASSWORD

WEBSITE	USER NAME	PASSWORD

WEBSITE	USER NAME	PASSWORD

Notes:

N

WEBSITE	USER NAME	PASSWORD

WEBSITE	USER NAME	PASSWORD

WEBSITE	USER NAME	PASSWORD

Notes:

N

WEBSITE	USER NAME	PASSWORD

WEBSITE	USER NAME	PASSWORD

WEBSITE	USER NAME	PASSWORD

Notes:

O

WEBSITE	USER NAME	PASSWORD

WEBSITE	USER NAME	PASSWORD

WEBSITE	USER NAME	PASSWORD

Notes:

O

WEBSITE USER NAME PASSWORD

WEBSITE USER NAME PASSWORD

WEBSITE USER NAME PASSWORD

Notes:

O

WEBSITE	USER NAME	PASSWORD

WEBSITE	USER NAME	PASSWORD

WEBSITE	USER NAME	PASSWORD

Notes:

P

WEBSITE	USER NAME	PASSWORD

WEBSITE	USER NAME	PASSWORD

WEBSITE	USER NAME	PASSWORD

Notes:

P

WEBSITE	USER NAME	PASSWORD

WEBSITE	USER NAME	PASSWORD

WEBSITE	USER NAME	PASSWORD

Notes:

P

WEBSITE	USER NAME	PASSWORD

WEBSITE	USER NAME	PASSWORD

WEBSITE	USER NAME	PASSWORD

Notes:

P

WEBSITE	USER NAME	PASSWORD

WEBSITE	USER NAME	PASSWORD

WEBSITE	USER NAME	PASSWORD

Notes:

O

WEBSITE	USER NAME	PASSWORD

WEBSITE	USER NAME	PASSWORD

WEBSITE	USER NAME	PASSWORD

Notes:

O

WEBSITE	USER NAME	PASSWORD

WEBSITE	USER NAME	PASSWORD

WEBSITE	USER NAME	PASSWORD

Notes:

O

WEBSITE	USER NAME	PASSWORD

WEBSITE	USER NAME	PASSWORD

WEBSITE	USER NAME	PASSWORD

Notes:

R

WEBSITE	USER NAME	PASSWORD

WEBSITE	USER NAME	PASSWORD

WEBSITE	USER NAME	PASSWORD

Notes:

R

WEBSITE	USER NAME	PASSWORD

WEBSITE	USER NAME	PASSWORD

WEBSITE	USER NAME	PASSWORD

Notes:

R

WEBSITE	USER NAME	PASSWORD

WEBSITE	USER NAME	PASSWORD

WEBSITE	USER NAME	PASSWORD

Notes:

R

WEBSITE	USER NAME	PASSWORD

WEBSITE	USER NAME	PASSWORD

WEBSITE	USER NAME	PASSWORD

Notes:

S

WEBSITE	USER NAME	PASSWORD

WEBSITE	USER NAME	PASSWORD

WEBSITE	USER NAME	PASSWORD

Notes:

S

WEBSITE	USER NAME	PASSWORD

WEBSITE	USER NAME	PASSWORD

WEBSITE	USER NAME	PASSWORD

Notes:

S

WEBSITE	USER NAME	PASSWORD

WEBSITE	USER NAME	PASSWORD

WEBSITE	USER NAME	PASSWORD

Notes:

S

WEBSITE	USER NAME	PASSWORD

WEBSITE	USER NAME	PASSWORD

WEBSITE	USER NAME	PASSWORD

Notes:

T

WEBSITE	USER NAME	PASSWORD

WEBSITE	USER NAME	PASSWORD

WEBSITE	USER NAME	PASSWORD

Notes:

T

WEBSITE	USER NAME	PASSWORD

WEBSITE	USER NAME	PASSWORD

WEBSITE	USER NAME	PASSWORD

Notes:

T

WEBSITE	USER NAME	PASSWORD

WEBSITE	USER NAME	PASSWORD

WEBSITE	USER NAME	PASSWORD

Notes:

T

WEBSITE	USER NAME	PASSWORD

WEBSITE	USER NAME	PASSWORD

WEBSITE	USER NAME	PASSWORD

Notes:

U

WEBSITE	USER NAME	PASSWORD

WEBSITE	USER NAME	PASSWORD

WEBSITE	USER NAME	PASSWORD

Notes:

U

WEBSITE	USER NAME	PASSWORD

WEBSITE	USER NAME	PASSWORD

WEBSITE	USER NAME	PASSWORD

Notes:

U

WEBSITE	USER NAME	PASSWORD

WEBSITE	USER NAME	PASSWORD

WEBSITE	USER NAME	PASSWORD

Notes:

V

WEBSITE	USER NAME	PASSWORD

WEBSITE	USER NAME	PASSWORD

WEBSITE	USER NAME	PASSWORD

Notes:

V

WEBSITE	USER NAME	PASSWORD

WEBSITE	USER NAME	PASSWORD

WEBSITE	USER NAME	PASSWORD

Notes:

V

WEBSITE	USER NAME	PASSWORD

WEBSITE	USER NAME	PASSWORD

WEBSITE	USER NAME	PASSWORD

Notes:

W

WEBSITE	USER NAME	PASSWORD

WEBSITE	USER NAME	PASSWORD

WEBSITE	USER NAME	PASSWORD

Notes:

W

WEBSITE	USER NAME	PASSWORD

WEBSITE	USER NAME	PASSWORD

WEBSITE	USER NAME	PASSWORD

Notes:

W

WEBSITE	USER NAME	PASSWORD

WEBSITE	USER NAME	PASSWORD

WEBSITE	USER NAME	PASSWORD

Notes:

X

WEBSITE	USER NAME	PASSWORD

WEBSITE	USER NAME	PASSWORD

WEBSITE	USER NAME	PASSWORD

Notes:

X

WEBSITE	USER NAME	PASSWORD

WEBSITE	USER NAME	PASSWORD

WEBSITE	USER NAME	PASSWORD

Notes:

X

WEBSITE	USER NAME	PASSWORD

WEBSITE	USER NAME	PASSWORD

WEBSITE	USER NAME	PASSWORD

Notes:

Y

WEBSITE	USER NAME	PASSWORD

WEBSITE	USER NAME	PASSWORD

WEBSITE	USER NAME	PASSWORD

Notes:

Y

WEBSITE	USER NAME	PASSWORD

WEBSITE	USER NAME	PASSWORD

WEBSITE	USER NAME	PASSWORD

Notes:

Y

WEBSITE	USER NAME	PASSWORD

WEBSITE	USER NAME	PASSWORD

WEBSITE	USER NAME	PASSWORD

Notes:

Y

WEBSITE	USER NAME	PASSWORD

WEBSITE	USER NAME	PASSWORD

WEBSITE	USER NAME	PASSWORD

Notes:

Z

WEBSITE	USER NAME	PASSWORD

WEBSITE	USER NAME	PASSWORD

WEBSITE	USER NAME	PASSWORD

Notes:

SUBSCRIPTIONS

WEBSITE:

Dollar Amount:

Subscription Renewal Date

Other:

WEBSITE:

Dollar Amount:

Subscription Renewal Date

Other:

WEBSITE:

Dollar Amount:

Subscription Renewal Date

Other:

WEBSITE:

Dollar Amount:

Subscription Renewal Date

Other:

WEBSITE:

Dollar Amount:

Subscription Renewal Date

Other:

WEBSITE:

Dollar Amount:

Subscription Renewal Date

Other:

WEBSITE:

Dollar Amount:

Subscription Renewal Date

Other:

WEBSITE:

Dollar Amount:

Subscription Renewal Date

Other:

SUBSCRIPTIONS

WEBSITE:

Dollar Amount: ....

Subscription Renewal Date ....

Other: ....

WEBSITE:

Dollar Amount: ....

Subscription Renewal Date ....

Other: ....

WEBSITE:

Dollar Amount: ....

Subscription Renewal Date ....

Other: ....

WEBSITE:

Dollar Amount: ....

Subscription Renewal Date ....

Other: ....

WEBSITE:

Dollar Amount: ....

Subscription Renewal Date ....

Other: ....

WEBSITE:

Dollar Amount: ....

Subscription Renewal Date ....

Other: ....

WEBSITE:

Dollar Amount: ....

Subscription Renewal Date ....

Other: ....

WEBSITE:

Dollar Amount: ....

Subscription Renewal Date ....

Other: ....

SUBSCRIPTIONS

WEBSITE:

Dollar Amount:

Subscription Renewal Date

Other:

WEBSITE:

Dollar Amount:

Subscription Renewal Date

Other:

WEBSITE:

Dollar Amount:

Subscription Renewal Date

Other:

WEBSITE:

Dollar Amount:

Subscription Renewal Date

Other:

WEBSITE:

Dollar Amount:

Subscription Renewal Date

Other:

WEBSITE:

Dollar Amount:

Subscription Renewal Date

Other:

WEBSITE:

Dollar Amount:

Subscription Renewal Date

Other:

WEBSITE:

Dollar Amount:

Subscription Renewal Date

Other:

SUBSCRIPTIONS

WEBSITE:

Dollar Amount:

Subscription Renewal Date

Other:

WEBSITE:

Dollar Amount:

Subscription Renewal Date

Other:

WEBSITE:

Dollar Amount:

Subscription Renewal Date

Other:

WEBSITE:

Dollar Amount:

Subscription Renewal Date

Other:

WEBSITE:

Dollar Amount:

Subscription Renewal Date

Other:

WEBSITE:

Dollar Amount:

Subscription Renewal Date

Other:

WEBSITE:

Dollar Amount:

Subscription Renewal Date

Other:

WEBSITE:

Dollar Amount:

Subscription Renewal Date

Other:

SUBSCRIPTIONS

WEBSITE:

Dollar Amount: ....

Subscription Renewal Date ....

Other: ....

WEBSITE:

Dollar Amount: ....

Subscription Renewal Date ....

Other: ....

WEBSITE:

Dollar Amount: ....

Subscription Renewal Date ....

Other: ....

WEBSITE:

Dollar Amount: ....

Subscription Renewal Date ....

Other: ....

WEBSITE:

Dollar Amount: ....

Subscription Renewal Date ....

Other: ....

WEBSITE:

Dollar Amount: ....

Subscription Renewal Date ....

Other: ....

WEBSITE:

Dollar Amount: ....

Subscription Renewal Date ....

Other: ....

WEBSITE:

Dollar Amount: ....

Subscription Renewal Date ....

Other: ....

SUBSCRIPTIONS

WEBSITE:

Dollar Amount:

Subscription Renewal Date

Other:

WEBSITE:

Dollar Amount:

Subscription Renewal Date

Other:

WEBSITE:

Dollar Amount:

Subscription Renewal Date

Other:

WEBSITE:

Dollar Amount:

Subscription Renewal Date

Other:

WEBSITE:

Dollar Amount:

Subscription Renewal Date

Other:

WEBSITE:

Dollar Amount:

Subscription Renewal Date

Other:

WEBSITE:

Dollar Amount:

Subscription Renewal Date

Other:

WEBSITE:

Dollar Amount:

Subscription Renewal Date

Other:

SUBSCRIPTIONS

WEBSITE:

Dollar Amount:

Subscription Renewal Date

Other:

WEBSITE:

Dollar Amount:

Subscription Renewal Date

Other:

WEBSITE:

Dollar Amount:

Subscription Renewal Date

Other:

WEBSITE:

Dollar Amount:

Subscription Renewal Date

Other:

WEBSITE:

Dollar Amount:

Subscription Renewal Date

Other:

WEBSITE:

Dollar Amount:

Subscription Renewal Date

Other:

WEBSITE:

Dollar Amount:

Subscription Renewal Date

Other:

WEBSITE:

Dollar Amount:

Subscription Renewal Date

Other:

SUBSCRIPTIONS

WEBSITE:

Dollar Amount:

Subscription Renewal Date

Other:

WEBSITE:

Dollar Amount:

Subscription Renewal Date

Other:

WEBSITE:

Dollar Amount:

Subscription Renewal Date

Other:

WEBSITE:

Dollar Amount:

Subscription Renewal Date

Other:

WEBSITE:

Dollar Amount:

Subscription Renewal Date

Other:

WEBSITE:

Dollar Amount:

Subscription Renewal Date

Other:

WEBSITE:

Dollar Amount:

Subscription Renewal Date

Other:

WEBSITE:

Dollar Amount:

Subscription Renewal Date

Other:

SUBSCRIPTIONS

WEBSITE:

Dollar Amount:

Subscription Renewal Date

Other:

WEBSITE:

Dollar Amount:

Subscription Renewal Date

Other:

WEBSITE:

Dollar Amount:

Subscription Renewal Date

Other:

WEBSITE:

Dollar Amount:

Subscription Renewal Date

Other:

WEBSITE:

Dollar Amount:

Subscription Renewal Date

Other:

WEBSITE:

Dollar Amount:

Subscription Renewal Date

Other:

WEBSITE:

Dollar Amount:

Subscription Renewal Date

Other:

WEBSITE:

Dollar Amount:

Subscription Renewal Date

Other:

SUBSCRIPTIONS

WEBSITE:

Dollar Amount: ....

Subscription Renewal Date ....

Other: ....

WEBSITE:

Dollar Amount: ....

Subscription Renewal Date ....

Other: ....

WEBSITE:

Dollar Amount: ....

Subscription Renewal Date ....

Other: ....

WEBSITE:

Dollar Amount: ....

Subscription Renewal Date ....

Other: ....

WEBSITE:

Dollar Amount: ....

Subscription Renewal Date ....

Other: ....

WEBSITE:

Dollar Amount: ....

Subscription Renewal Date ....

Other: ....

WEBSITE:

Dollar Amount: ....

Subscription Renewal Date ....

Other: ....

WEBSITE:

Dollar Amount: ....

Subscription Renewal Date ....

Other: ....

SUBSCRIPTIONS

WEBSITE:

Dollar Amount: ....

Subscription Renewal Date ....

Other: ....

WEBSITE:

Dollar Amount: ....

Subscription Renewal Date ....

Other: ....

WEBSITE:

Dollar Amount: ....

Subscription Renewal Date ....

Other: ....

WEBSITE:

Dollar Amount: ....

Subscription Renewal Date ....

Other: ....

WEBSITE:

Dollar Amount: ....

Subscription Renewal Date ....

Other: ....

WEBSITE:

Dollar Amount: ....

Subscription Renewal Date ....

Other: ....

WEBSITE:

Dollar Amount: ....

Subscription Renewal Date ....

Other: ....

WEBSITE:

Dollar Amount: ....

Subscription Renewal Date ....

Other: ....

SUBSCRIPTIONS

WEBSITE:

Dollar Amount: ....

Subscription Renewal Date ....

Other: ....

WEBSITE:

Dollar Amount: ....

Subscription Renewal Date ....

Other: ....

WEBSITE:

Dollar Amount: ....

Subscription Renewal Date ....

Other: ....

WEBSITE:

Dollar Amount: ....

Subscription Renewal Date ....

Other: ....

WEBSITE:

Dollar Amount: ....

Subscription Renewal Date ....

Other: ....

WEBSITE:

Dollar Amount: ....

Subscription Renewal Date ....

Other: ....

WEBSITE:

Dollar Amount: ....

Subscription Renewal Date ....

Other: ....

WEBSITE:

Dollar Amount: ....

Subscription Renewal Date ....

Other: ....

SUBSCRIPTIONS

WEBSITE:

Dollar Amount:

Subscription Renewal Date

Other:

WEBSITE:

Dollar Amount:

Subscription Renewal Date

Other:

WEBSITE:

Dollar Amount:

Subscription Renewal Date

Other:

WEBSITE:

Dollar Amount:

Subscription Renewal Date

Other:

WEBSITE:

Dollar Amount:

Subscription Renewal Date

Other:

WEBSITE:

Dollar Amount:

Subscription Renewal Date

Other:

WEBSITE:

Dollar Amount:

Subscription Renewal Date

Other:

WEBSITE:

Dollar Amount:

Subscription Renewal Date

Other:

SUBSCRIPTIONS

WEBSITE:

Dollar Amount:

Subscription Renewal Date

Other:

WEBSITE:

Dollar Amount:

Subscription Renewal Date

Other:

WEBSITE:

Dollar Amount:

Subscription Renewal Date

Other:

WEBSITE:

Dollar Amount:

Subscription Renewal Date

Other:

WEBSITE:

Dollar Amount:

Subscription Renewal Date

Other:

WEBSITE:

Dollar Amount:

Subscription Renewal Date

Other:

WEBSITE:

Dollar Amount:

Subscription Renewal Date

Other:

WEBSITE:

Dollar Amount:

Subscription Renewal Date

Other:

SUBSCRIPTIONS

WEBSITE:

Dollar Amount: ....

Subscription Renewal Date ....

Other: ....

WEBSITE:

Dollar Amount: ....

Subscription Renewal Date ....

Other: ....

WEBSITE:

Dollar Amount: ....

Subscription Renewal Date ....

Other: ....

WEBSITE:

Dollar Amount: ....

Subscription Renewal Date ....

Other: ....

WEBSITE:

Dollar Amount: ....

Subscription Renewal Date ....

Other: ....

WEBSITE:

Dollar Amount: ....

Subscription Renewal Date ....

Other: ....

WEBSITE:

Dollar Amount: ....

Subscription Renewal Date ....

Other: ....

WEBSITE:

Dollar Amount: ....

Subscription Renewal Date ....

Other: ....

SUBSCRIPTIONS

WEBSITE:

Dollar Amount: ....

Subscription Renewal Date ....

Other: ....

WEBSITE:

Dollar Amount: ....

Subscription Renewal Date ....

Other: ....

WEBSITE:

Dollar Amount: ....

Subscription Renewal Date ....

Other: ....

WEBSITE:

Dollar Amount: ....

Subscription Renewal Date ....

Other: ....

WEBSITE:

Dollar Amount: ....

Subscription Renewal Date ....

Other: ....

WEBSITE:

Dollar Amount: ....

Subscription Renewal Date ....

Other: ....

WEBSITE:

Dollar Amount: ....

Subscription Renewal Date ....

Other: ....

WEBSITE:

Dollar Amount: ....

Subscription Renewal Date ....

Other: ....

SUBSCRIPTIONS

WEBSITE:

Dollar Amount: ....

Subscription Renewal Date ....

Other: ....

WEBSITE:

Dollar Amount: ....

Subscription Renewal Date ....

Other: ....

WEBSITE:

Dollar Amount: ....

Subscription Renewal Date ....

Other: ....

WEBSITE:

Dollar Amount: ....

Subscription Renewal Date ....

Other: ....

WEBSITE:

Dollar Amount: ....

Subscription Renewal Date ....

Other: ....

WEBSITE:

Dollar Amount: ....

Subscription Renewal Date ....

Other: ....

WEBSITE:

Dollar Amount: ....

Subscription Renewal Date ....

Other: ....

WEBSITE:

Dollar Amount: ....

Subscription Renewal Date ....

Other: ....

SUBSCRIPTIONS

WEBSITE:

Dollar Amount:

Subscription Renewal Date

Other:

WEBSITE:

Dollar Amount:

Subscription Renewal Date

Other:

WEBSITE:

Dollar Amount:

Subscription Renewal Date

Other:

WEBSITE:

Dollar Amount:

Subscription Renewal Date

Other:

WEBSITE:

Dollar Amount:

Subscription Renewal Date

Other:

WEBSITE:

Dollar Amount:

Subscription Renewal Date

Other:

WEBSITE:

Dollar Amount:

Subscription Renewal Date

Other:

WEBSITE:

Dollar Amount:

Subscription Renewal Date

Other:

SUBSCRIPTIONS

WEBSITE:

Dollar Amount: ....

Subscription
Renewal Date ....

Other: ....

WEBSITE:

Dollar Amount: ....

Subscription
Renewal Date ....

Other: ....

WEBSITE:

Dollar Amount: ....

Subscription
Renewal Date ....

Other: ....

WEBSITE:

Dollar Amount: ....

Subscription
Renewal Date ....

Other: ....

WEBSITE:

Dollar Amount: ....

Subscription
Renewal Date ....

Other: ....

WEBSITE:

Dollar Amount: ....

Subscription
Renewal Date ....

Other: ....

WEBSITE:

Dollar Amount: ....

Subscription
Renewal Date ....

Other: ....

WEBSITE:

Dollar Amount: ....

Subscription
Renewal Date ....

Other: ....

SUBSCRIPTIONS

WEBSITE:

Dollar Amount:

Subscription Renewal Date

Other:

WEBSITE:

Dollar Amount:

Subscription Renewal Date

Other:

WEBSITE:

Dollar Amount:

Subscription Renewal Date

Other:

WEBSITE:

Dollar Amount:

Subscription Renewal Date

Other:

WEBSITE:

Dollar Amount:

Subscription Renewal Date

Other:

WEBSITE:

Dollar Amount:

Subscription Renewal Date

Other:

WEBSITE:

Dollar Amount:

Subscription Renewal Date

Other:

WEBSITE:

Dollar Amount:

Subscription Renewal Date

Other:

Made in the USA
Monee, IL
04 November 2026

67387892R00069